SCHOLASTIC

EXTRA PRACTICE

Struggling Readers

HIGH-FREQUENCY WORDS

Linda Ward Beech

New York • Toronto • London • Auckland • Sydney
Mexico City • New Delhi • Hong Kong • Buenos Aires

Teaching *Resources*

Editor: Mela Ottaiano
Cover design: Brian LaRossa
Interior design: Melinda Belter
Interior illustrations: Teresa Anderko

ISBN-13: 978-0-545-12410-2
ISBN-10: 0-545-12410-7

26   40   23/0

Contents

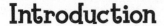

Introduction

Learning to read is *the* goal for all students, but unfortunately success is not a given. Many students, for many reasons, find reading an enormous challenge. Despite excellent reading programs, dedicated teachers, and various kinds of interventions, far too many students emerge from the primary grades as struggling readers. One way in which to help these students is through additional practice with high-frequency words.

High-frequency words are often called *sight words* because readers need to know them at a glance. Since 100 high-frequency words make up about half of all the words found in books, it is crucial for students to be able to read and spell them. Although many of these words are *function* words that carry little meaning, they greatly affect the flow and coherence of a text.

One of the reasons high-frequency words cause problems is because many of these words are not easily decodable and do not follow the usual sound-spelling relationships. For example, the words *hat, bed,* and *play* follow common rules of phonics, while the words *has, none,* and *could* do not. When students can identify high-frequency words quickly and accurately, their reading fluency increases, and their reading comprehension improves.

By offering opportunities to review or learn anew basic sight words, the lessons in this book help students develop reading fluency. You can use the lessons in the sequence given or choose those needed to address specific words that give students problems.

Lesson Organization

Each lesson is three pages long and focuses on 10 words.

The first lesson page includes:

- 10 common sight words

- a visual activity involving the words

- an exercise that focuses on the letters or phonics in each word

- another exercise

The second page includes:

- a cloze exercise

- two other exercises, including rhyming, word meaning, synonyms, antonyms, homophones, syllables, verb tense, and word endings

The third page includes:

- a word-meaning exercise, such as answering riddles

- a comprehension passage with questions, or a word puzzle

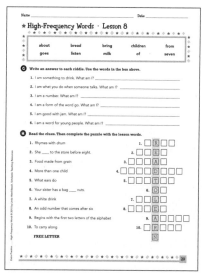

Ways to Make the Most of the Lessons

- Use the lessons in the classroom for extra practice during regular reading time or as individual assignments. Send the lessons home for students to do as homework or to complete with an adult.

- Review, review, review. You'll find that many words from previous lessons appear in the cloze activity (Exercise D) and the reading comprehension passage (Exercise H) in each lesson.

- Use the lessons to expand students' understanding of grammar. Some exercises refer to verb tense; others incorporate the use of inflected endings.

- Encourage students to write complete sentences when they respond to the reading passages in Exercise H.

- Create word lists from each lesson. Students can use them in word sorts, on word walls, in writing assignments, or in reader's journals.

- Build on lessons with riddles. Challenge students to write their own riddles about the words in a lesson.

- Keep observation charts to monitor progress.

★ High-Frequency Words · Lesson 1

answer	by	find	has	is
school	sister	this	what	your

A Read the lesson words above. Write a word that fits each shape.

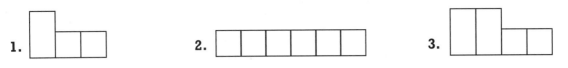

1.　　　　　　　　　　2.　　　　　　　　　　3.

4.　　　　　　　　　　5.　　　　　　　　　　6.

B On another sheet of paper make a shape for each word you did not use.
Write the words below.

1. _____   3. _____

2. _____   4. _____

C Write a lesson word for each clue.

1. Write a word with two *o's*.   _____

2. Write a word that begins with *th*.   _____

3. Write a word that rhymes with *eye*.   _____

4. Write a word that begins with *wh*.   _____

5. Write a word that begins like *you*.   _____

6. Write a word that ends in *nd*.   _____

7. Write a word with the word *as* in it.   _____

8. Write a word that rhymes with *fizz*.   _____

9. Write two words that end with *er*.   _____ _____

★ High-Frequency Words · Lesson 1

answer	by	find	has	is
school	sister	this	what	your

D **Read each sentence. Find and circle the word that best fits.**

1. Is _____ a school?   a. **what**   b. **this**   c. **have**

2. This is _____ school.   a. **your**   b. **by**   c. **answer**

3. What is your _____ ?   a. **this**   b. **answer**   c. **find**

4. Your sister is _____ the school.   a. **has**   b. **answer**   c. **by**

5. Your sister _____ this answer.   a. **this**   b. **what**   c. **has**

6. _____ your school.   a. **Find**   b. **Has**   c. **What**

7. What _____ the answer?   a. **this**   b. **is**   c. **by**

8. This is your _____ .   a. **sister**   b. **has**   c. **find**

9. Find this _____ .   a. **is**   b. **your**   c. **answer**

10. Your sister is in _____ .   a. **answer**   b. **school**   c. **find**

E **Draw a line from each word in the top row to its antonym in the bottom row. (An *antonym* is a word that has the opposite meaning from another word.)**

1. sister   2. your   3. find   4. answer   5. is   6. has

a. **hasn't**   b. **lose**   c. **ask**   d. **isn't**   e. **brother**   f. **my**

F **Write the present tense of each verb.**

1. was _____   2. had _____   3. found _____

Name _____   Date _____

★ High-Frequency Words · Lesson 1

answer	by	find	has	is
school	sister	this	what	your

G **Write *yes* or *no* to answer each question.**

1. Do fish swim in a school? _____

2. Does *answer* mean "reply"? _____

3. Is your sister a relative? _____

4. Does *by* mean "shop"? _____

5. Does *find* mean "seek"? _____

H **Read the clues. Then complete the puzzle with the lesson words.**

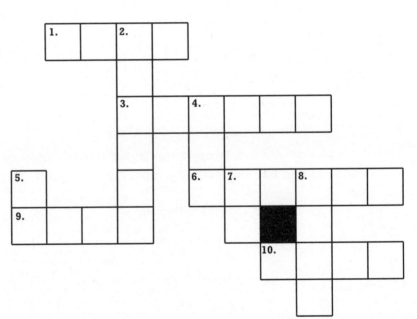

ACROSS

1. a word that starts a question

3. a place where you learn

6. a daughter of your parents

9. belonging to you

10. look for

DOWN

2. what you do when asked a question

4. rhymes with *jazz*

5. at or near

7. She _____ here.

8. rhymes with *miss*

★ High-Frequency Words · Lesson 2

been	call	eight	house	letter
new	on	said	the	why

A Write a word from the box for each picture.

1.

2.

3. *8*

_____   _____   _____

B Write a lesson word that fits in each shape.

1. 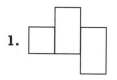   2. 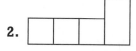   3. 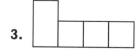   4. ☐☐

5. ☐☐☐   6.    7. ☐☐

C Write a lesson word for each clue.

1. Write a word that begins with *wh*.   _____

2. Write a word that has the word *bee* in it.   _____

3. Write a word that rhymes with *you*.   _____

4. Write a word that ends in *d*.   _____

5. Write a word that sounds like *ate*.   _____

6. Write a word that has two letters.   _____

7. Write two words that end in silent *e*.   _____   _____

8. Write two words that have double
   consonants.   _____   _____

★ High-Frequency Words · Lesson 2

been	call	eight	house	letter
new	on	said	the	why

D **Read each sentence. Find and circle the word that best fits.**

1. Jim said he will _____ us. a. **new** b. **call** c. **why**

2. She has _____ at the house. a. **been** b. **is** c. **letter**

3. I will answer your _____ . a. **said** b. **house** c. **letter**

4. _____ did you call the school? a. **Said** b. **Why** c. **New**

5. This is my new _____ . a. **eight** b. **house** c. **the**

6. He _____ to come by at eight. a. **been** b. **new** c. **said**

7. She has a _____ sister. a. **call** b. **why** c. **new**

8. What is _____ the cat? a. **on** b. **said** c. **been**

9. Find _____ house. a. **on** b. **the** c. **by**

10. She got _____ letters. a. **house** b. **on** c. **eight**

E **Circle the correct homophone for each word meaning. (A *homophone* is a word that sounds like another word but has a different meaning and a different spelling.)**

1. opposite of old   new   knew

2. a verb form   been   bin

F **Write a word from the house that rhymes with each word below.**

1. said _____   4. eight _____

2. letter _____   5. house _____

3. why _____   6. call _____

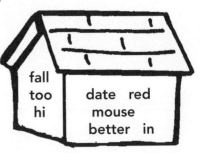

fall too hi date red mouse better in

★ High-Frequency Words · Lesson 2

been	call	eight	house	letter
new	on	said	the	why

G **Write an answer to each riddle. Use the words in the box above.**

1. I am a number. What am I? _____

2. I am the past tense of *say*. What am I? _____

3. I am a place to live. What am I? _____

4. I begin questions. What am I? _____

5. I am one of 26 in the alphabet. What am I? _____

6. I rhyme with *all*. What am I? _____

H **Read the paragraphs, then answer the questions.**

> Pam finds eight new letters at the house. Her sister
> Lee has been by. Why?
> What is on Lee's mind? Pam calls Lee.
> "What is in your letters?"
> Lee said, "Open the letters. This is the way you will
> find out!"

1. Who likes to write letters? _____

2. How many letters did Pam get? _____

3. Where did Pam find the letters? _____

4. What did Pam do? _____

5. How can Pam find out what is in the letters? _____

6. What do you think is in the letters? _____

★ High-Frequency Words · Lesson 3

and	both	circle	family	go
pencil	she	talk	use	when

A Write a word from the box for each picture.

1.  _____

2.  _____

3.  _____

4.  _____

B Write a lesson word that fits in each shape.

1.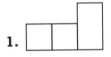

2.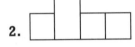

3.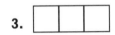

4.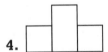

5.

6.

C Write a lesson word for each clue.

1. Write a word that ends in *ly*.   _____

2. Write a word that begins like *pen*.   _____

3. Write a word that begins with *wh*.   _____

4. Write a word that rhymes with *me*.   _____

5. Write a word that has two sounds for "c."   _____

6. Write a word that ends with *lk*.   _____

7. Write two words that begin with a vowel.   _____ _____

8. Write two words with long /o/.   _____ _____

★ High-Frequency Words · Lesson 3

and	both	circle	family	go
pencil	she	talk	use	when

D **Read each sentence. Find and circle the word that best fits.**

1. What is in the _____ ?   a. **use**   b. **both**   c. **circle**

2. Is this your _____ ?   a. **eight**   b. **family**   c. **when**

3. We will _____ to school.   a. **on**   b. **by**   c. **go**

4. Jane _____ Ned are here.   a. **and**   b. **been**   c. **has**

5. They are _____ new at school.   a. **your**   b. **both**   c. **and**

6. _____ will you go to the house?   a. **What**   b. **Find**   c. **When**

7. This _____ is red.   a. **pencil**   b. **answer**   c. **eight**

8. Can we _____ a pencil for the test?   a. **has**   b. **use**   c. **by**

9. We will _____ at school.   a. **circle**   b. **said**   c. **talk**

10. Is _____ your sister?   a. **the**   b. **she**   c. **new**

E **Write a word from the pencil that rhymes with each word below.**

hen   walk   new   he   why   hand   so   call

1. and _____   2. go _____   3. when _____

4. talk _____   5. she _____

F **Write yes or no to answer each question.**

1. Does *talk* mean "speak"? _____   3. Is a sister part of a family? _____

2. Does a circle have points? _____   4. Can you use a pencil in school? _____

★ High-Frequency Words · Lesson 3

and	both	circle	family	go
pencil	she	talk	use	when

G **Write an answer to each riddle. Use the words in the box above.**

1. I stand for a girl's name in a sentence. What am I? _____

2. I write on paper. What am I? _____

3. I link two words in a sentence. What am I? _____

4. I have no corners. What am I? _____

5. I am a group of relatives. What am I? _____

6. I am what you do on the phone. What am I? _____

H **Read the paragraphs, then answer the questions.**

The Tell family has a new house. Both Paul and Jill will go to a new school. Jill has not ever been to school. She and Paul talk.

"When will we go? When? When? When?" Jill runs in a circle.

"Can I use my new pencil at school?"

Paul smiles. "When you go to school, you will use it a lot."

1. Who has just moved? _____

2. Who is older, Paul or Jill? _____

3. About how old is Jill? _____

4. Who is excited about school? _____

5. What does Jill have? _____

6. What will Jill do with her pencil? _____

★ High-Frequency Words · Lesson 4

are	city	do	for	have
help	month	read	teacher	with

A Write a word from the box for each picture.

1.

2.

3.

_____   _____   _____

B Read the lesson words above. Write a word that fits each shape.

1.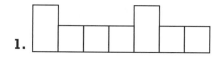

2.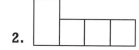

3.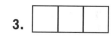

4.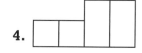

5.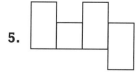

6.

7.

C Write a lesson word for each clue.

1. Write a word with *ch* in it.   _____

2. Write a word that sounds like *dew*.   _____

3. Write a word that ends in *y*.   _____

4. Write a word that sounds like the letter *r*.   _____

5. Write a word that rhymes with *seed*.   _____

6. Write a word that sounds like *four*.   _____

7. Write two words that begin with *h*.   _____ _____

8. Write two words that end in *th*.   _____ _____

★ High-Frequency Words · Lesson 4

are	city	do	for	have
help	month	read	teacher	with

D **Read each sentence. Find and circle the word that best fits.**

1. Is your house in the ____ ?   a. **sister**   b. **city**   c. **month**

2. ____ you in school?   a. **Are**   b. **And**   c. **Is**

3. What ____ is it?   a. **month**   b. **eight**   c. **circle**

4. Is this what you ____ in school?   a. **go**   b. **do**   c. **by**

5. Will you ____ to your family?   a. **have**   b. **said**   c. **read**

6. Your ____ is new at this school.   a. **house**   b. **teacher**   c. **city**

7. She will ____ you find a pencil.   a. **help**   b. **when**   c. **talk**

8. Go to the house ____ your sister.   a. **both**   b. **with**   c. **why**

9. Ask your family ____ help.   a. **by**   b. **for**   c. **has**

10. You ____ to answer this letter.   a. **talk**   b. **been**   c. **have**

E **Write the present tense of each verb.**

1. were _____   2. did _____   3. helped _____

F **Read the word in the first column. Underline the word in the row that begins the same way.**

1. city   circle   call   both

2. for   off   torn   form

3. month   none   new   mother

4. read   said   reed   have

5. with   wit   vim   in

6. teacher   leak   fee   tea

★ High-Frequency Words · Lesson 4

are	city	do	for	have
help	month	read	teacher	with

G Draw a line from each word on the left to its antonym on the right. (An *antonym* is a word that has the opposite meaning from another word.)

1. with   a. student

2. city   b. haven't

3. do   c. don't

4. teacher   d. aren't

5. have   e. without

6. are   f. country

H Read the paragraphs, then answer the questions.

Jen and Sue are sisters. Both of them have lots of books. Jen can read well, but Sue is new at it. Jen sits with her sister to help her with a book. She is a good teacher for Sue.

"What letters do you see in city?" Jen says.

Sue can read all the letters.

Jen is happy. "I have been your teacher for a month, and see how well you do!"

1. What do the sisters have? _____

2. Who reads well? _____

3. How does Jen help Sue? _____

4. Why might Sue be new at reading? _____

5. What might the book be about? _____

6. Why is Jen a good teacher? _____

★ High-Frequency Words · Lesson 5

could	each	his	light	money
our	store	that	they	who

A Write a word from the box for each picture.

 1. _____

 2. _____

 3. _____

B Read the lesson words above. Write a word that fits each shape.

1.

2.

3.

4.

5.

6.

7.

C Write a lesson word for each clue.

1. Write a word that ends like *would*. _____

2. Write a word that rhymes with *is*. _____

3. Write a word that begins with *st*. _____

4. Write a word that rhymes with *honey*. _____

5. Write a word that begins with *wh*. _____

6. Write a word that rhymes with *bite*. _____

7. Write two words that begin with vowels. _____ _____

8. Write two words that begin with *th*. _____ _____

★ High-Frequency Words · Lesson 5

could	each	his	light	money
our	store	that	they	who

D **Read each sentence. Find and circle the word that best fits.**

1. Dave will use ____ pencil to mark the circles. a. **they** b. **both** c. **his**

2. The ____ is on in the house. a. **light** b. **money** c. **store**

3. Ben and his sister ____ have a bike. a. **our** b. **each** c. **she**

4. Will ____ go to the store in the city? a. **your** b. **they** c. **our**

5. She ____ read to the teacher. a. **have** b. **are** c. **could**

6. ____ has a pencil for Maria? a. **What** b. **Who** c. **His**

7. Do you have ____ at the house? a. **call** b. **month** c. **money**

8. She will ____ the letter. a. **that** b. **both** c. **read**

9. Go to the ____ by the school. a. **eight** b. **store** c. **answer**

10. This is ____ new house. a. **for** b. **use** c. **our**

E **Draw a line from each word in the top row to its antonym in the bottom row. (An _antonym_ is a word that has the opposite meaning from another word.)**

1. each 2. they 3. our 4. his 5. could 6. light

a. **dark** b. **hers** c. **couldn't** d. **every** e. **we** f. **your**

F **Write _yes_ or _no_ to answer each question.**

1. Can _store_ mean "put away"? _____

2. Does _could_ have a silent letter? _____

3. Does _his_ mean "belonging to a girl"? _____

4. Can _light_ mean "not heavy"? _____

Name _____   Date _____

★ High-Frequency Words · Lesson 5

could	each	his	light	money
our	store	that	they	who

G **Write an answer to each riddle. Use the words in the box above.**

1. I am used to buy things. What am I? _____

2. I have the word *hat* in me. What am I? _____

3. I rhyme with *day*. What am I? _____

4. I am a place where you shop. What am I? _____

5. I am what you read by. What am I? _____

6. I am what an owl says. What am I? _____

H **Read the paragraphs, then answer the questions.**

Bob's dad has a shop in the city. This month Bob has no school,
so his dad said that Bob could help in the store. Bob likes that a lot.
They go to the city each day when it is just light out.

Our family likes to shop at this store. When I have money, I go too.
Who helps me shop? You said it—the answer is Bob!

1. What does Bob do when there is no school? _____

2. How does he feel about that? _____

3. Who works with Bob? _____

4. Where is the store? _____

5. When does Bob get to the store each day? _____

6. What does Bob do in the store? _____

Name _____ Date _____

★ High-Frequency Words · Lesson 6

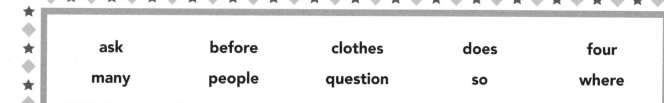

ask	before	clothes	does	four
many	people	question	so	where

A Write a word from the box for each picture.

1. **?**   2. **4**   3.    4.

_____   _____   _____   _____

B A syllable is a word part that has a vowel sound in it. Write each lesson word in the correct column on the chart to show how many syllables it has.

One Syllable	_____ _____ _____
	_____ _____ _____
Two Syllables	_____ _____ _____
	_____ _____ _____

C Write a lesson word for each clue.

1. Write a word that ends in *y*. _____

2. Write a word that ends in *sk*. _____

3. Write a word that begins with *wh*. _____

4. Write a word that has two *p*'s. _____

5. Write a word that sounds like *sew*. _____

6. Write a word that begins with *qu*. _____

7. Write a word that rhymes with *fuzz*. _____

8. Write a word that begins with *cl*. _____

9. Write two words that have a sound like *for*. _____ _____

ask	before	clothes	does	four
many	people	question	so	where

D **Read each sentence. Find and circle the word that best fits.**

1. Talk to Mom _____ you go to the city.   a. **before**   b. **both**   c. **been**

2. His _____ got wet in the rain.   a. **circles**   b. **calls**   c. **clothes**

3. Did you _____ your sister to go with you?   a. **are**   b. **and**   c. **ask**

4. When _____ your school open?   a. **four**   b. **does**   c. **has**

5. _____ is the light in this store?   a. **When**   b. **Why**   c. **Where**

6. She has _____ books to read.   a. **money**   b. **many**   c. **each**

7. Eight _____ are in the store.   a. **people**   b. **months**   c. **answers**

8. What _____ did you ask the teacher?   a. **pencil**   b. **clothes**   c. **question**

9. I will call you _____ we can talk.   a. **so**   b. **go**   c. **do**

10. They have _____ pets in that house.   a. **for**   b. **on**   c. **four**

E **Write a word from the dress that rhymes with each word below.**

1. where _____

2. people _____

3. clothes _____

4. ask _____

5. four _____

6. so _____

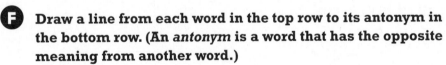

mask
go
care
steeple
light   hose
more   who

F **Draw a line from each word in the top row to its antonym in the bottom row. (An *antonym* is a word that has the opposite meaning from another word.)**

1. many   2. before   3. does   4. question

a. **doesn't**   b. **answer**   c. **few**   d. **after**

★ High-Frequency Words · Lesson 6

ask	before	clothes	does	four
many	people	question	so	where

G **Each word below is found in a word in the box. Write the word from the box.**

1. man _____

2. as _____

3. here _____

4. for _____

5. our _____

6. lot _____

H **Read the paragraphs, then answer the questions.**

> It was time for school, and Al could not find his clothes.
>
> "Where are my pants?" he said. "Where are my socks? Where is my coat? Where is my hat?"
>
> Ruth said, "Why do you ask so many questions? You don't need help to find your clothes. Just look!"
>
> "He does need help," said Mom. "Al has lost four things. Before he can go to school, he must find them."
>
> "If you people help me," said Al, "I will not ask so many questions."
>
> "AND you can go to school," said Ruth.

1. What has Al lost? _____

2. Who doesn't want to help him? _____

3. Who thinks he needs help? _____

4. What does Mom want? _____

5. Why do you think Al has lost so many things? _____

6. Do you think Al has ever lost things before? Why? _____

★ High-Frequency Words · Lesson 7

address	buy	come	head	little
one	should	table	walk	work

A **Write a word from the box for each picture.**

1.    2. **1**   3.   4.

_____   _____   _____   _____

B **Circle each ending that can be added to the word to make a new word. Write the new word or words.**

1. walk   s   ed   est   _____ _____ _____

2. work   er   ing   ed   _____ _____ _____

3. buy   ed   s   ing   _____ _____ _____

4. come   est   ed   s   _____ _____ _____

C **Write a lesson word for each clue.**

1. Write a word that rhymes with *bed*.   _____

2. Write a word that ends in *rk*.   _____

3. Write a word that sounds like *won*.   _____

4. Write a word that begins with *sh*.   _____

5. Write a word that ends in *lk*.   _____

6. Write a word that sounds like *by*.   _____

7. Write a word with two sets of double letters.   _____

8. Write a word that rhymes with *some*.   _____

9. Write two words that end with *le*.   _____ _____

★ High-Frequency Words · Lesson 7

address	buy	come	head	little
one	should	table	walk	work

D Read each sentence. Find and circle the word that best fits.

1. What is your new ____ ?   a. **light**   b. **address**   c. **clothes**

2. Where does your sister ____ ?   a. **said**   b. **ask**   c. **work**

3. Will you ____ to the city with me?   a. **read**   b. **come**   c. **find**

4. They ____ talk to his family.   a. **before**   b. **should**   c. **has**

5. She has ____ money.   a. **little**   b. **use**   c. **been**

6. You can read at this ____ .   a. **table**   b. **circle**   c. **month**

7. Is ____ of the pencils for me?   a. **eight**   b. **new**   c. **one**

8. Does your teacher ____ to school?   a. **help**   b. **what**   c. **walk**

9. Is she the ____ of your school?   a. **light**   b. **head**   c. **call**

10. When will you ____ a new light?   a. **buy**   b. **help**   c. **talk**

E Draw a line from each word in the top row to its antonym in the bottom row. (An *antonym* is a word that has the opposite meaning from another word.)

1. little   2. work   3. buy   4. come   5. should   6. head

a. **foot**   b. **shouldn't**   c. **big**   d. **sell**   e. **play**   f. **go**

F Write the missing vowels in each word below.

1. ____ ddr ____ ss   2. ____ n ____   3. t ____ bl ____   4. w ____ lk

★ High-Frequency Words · Lesson 7

address	buy	come	head	little
one	should	table	walk	work

G **Write *yes* or *no* to answer each question.**

1. Does *little* mean "small"? _____

2. Should you stand on a table? _____

3. Can you buy one pencil? _____

4. Is an address on a letter? _____

5. Can people walk to work? _____

6. Does your head come off? _____

H **Read the paragraphs, then answer the questions.**

A new store opened near Ann's house.

"What is the address of that store?" she asked Lisa. "I will walk to it before I go to work."

"Can I come with you?" said Lisa. "I should buy clothes, too. I could use a light top."

At the store, the girls looked at hats that were on a table.

"This one is too little," said Ann, "or my head is too big!"

"This store has many hats," said Lisa. "You should find one that fits."

1. Where is the new store? _____

2. Who has the address of the store? _____

3. Why are the girls going to the store? _____

4. What does Ann try on? _____

5. Do you think Ann will find a hat or not? Explain. _____

6. What do you think the girls will look at next? _____

★ High-Frequency Words · Lesson 8

about	bread	bring	children	from
goes	listen	milk	of	seven

A Write a word from the box for each picture.

1. 7

2.

3.

4.

_____   _____   _____   _____

B A syllable is a word part that has a vowel sound. Write each lesson word in the correct column on the chart to show how many syllables it has.

One Syllable

_____ _____ _____

_____ _____ _____

Two Syllables

_____ _____

_____ _____

C Write a lesson word for each clue.

1. Write a word that begins with *fr*.   _____

2. Write a word that ends in *lk*.   _____

3. Write a word that begins with *ch*.   _____

4. Write a word that rhymes with *toes*.   _____

5. Write a word that has the word *out* in it.   _____

6. Write a word that rhymes with *eleven*.   _____

7. Write a word that has two letters.   _____

8. Write a word that has the word *list* in it.   _____

9. Write two words that begin with *br*.   _____ _____

★ High-Frequency Words · Lesson 8

about	bread	bring	children	from
goes	listen	milk	of	seven

D **Read each sentence. Find and circle the word that best fits.**

1. Who will ____ the children to school?   a. **goes**   b. **does**   c. **bring**

2. Did you ____ to what your teacher said?   a. **talk**   b. **listen**   c. **read**

3. She was ill ____ days this month.   a. **little**   b. **light**   c. **seven**

4. What is this new book ____ ?   a. **work**   b. **about**   c. **do**

5. The ____ ask many questions.   a. **children**   b. **sister**   c. **family**

6. Jay ____ to the city before seven.   a. **goes**   b. **does**   c. **been**

7. Go to the store for some ____ .   a. **people**   b. **light**   c. **bread**

8. She used all ____ her money to buy clothes.   a. **for**   b. **of**   c. **on**

9. This letter is ____ my sister's house.   a. **with**   b. **both**   c. **from**

10. Each day, the children have ____ at school.   a. **milk**   b. **money**   c. **month**

E **Write yes or no to answer each question.**

1. Does seven come before eight? _____

2. Does milk come from a cow? _____

3. Can you listen to bread? _____

4. Is the word *children* plural? _____

5. Can a table be made from wood? _____

6. Is it winter in the month of May? _____

F **Write the present tense of each verb.**

1. brought   2. went   3. listened

_____   _____   _____

★ High-Frequency Words · Lesson 8

about	bread	bring	children	from
goes	listen	milk	of	seven

G **Write an answer to each riddle. Use the words in the box above.**

1. I am something to drink. What am I? _____

2. I am what you do when someone talks. What am I? _____

3. I am a number. What am I? _____

4. I am a form of the word go. What am I? _____

5. I am good with jam. What am I? _____

6. I am a word for young people. What am I? _____

H **Read the clues. Then complete the puzzle with the lesson words.**

1. Rhymes with *drum*

2. She ____ to the store before eight.

3. Food made from grain

4. More than one child

5. What ears do

6. Your sister has a bag ____ nuts.

7. A white drink

8. An odd number that comes after six

9. Begins with the first two letters of the alphabet

10. To carry along

★ High-Frequency Words · Lesson 9

again	brother	door	happen	hundred
jump	paper	remain	some	was

A Write a word from the box for each picture.

1. 100   2.   3.   4.

_____   _____   _____   _____

B Circle each ending that can be added to the word to make a new word. Write the new word or words.

1. paper   *ed*   *ing*   *s*   _____ _____ _____

2. happen   *ed*   *s*   *ing*   _____ _____ _____

3. remain   *ing*   *s*   *ed*   _____ _____ _____

4. jump   *s*   *ed*   *ing*   _____ _____ _____

C Write a lesson word for each clue.

1. Write a word that ends in *mp*.   _____

2. Write a word that sounds like *sum*.   _____

3. Write a word that begins with *br*.   _____

4. Write a word that has the word *gain* in it.   _____

5. Write a word that rhymes with *fuzz*.   _____

6. Write a word that has two *p's*.   _____

7. Write a word that has the word *main* in it.   _____

8. Write a word that has double *o's*.   _____

9. Write two words that begin with *h*.   _____ _____

★ High-Frequency Words · Lesson 9

| again | brother | door | happen | hundred |
| jump | paper | remain | some | was |

D Read each sentence. Find and circle the word that best fits.

1. She got up to get ____ milk.   a. **eight**   b. **some**   c. **each**

2. The light ____ on in the house.   a. **was**   b. **been**   c. **has**

3. Is your ____ seven or eight?   a. **family**   b. **teacher**   c. **brother**

4. The teacher asked her to read ____ .   a. **again**   b. **about**   c. **with**

5. He will walk you to the ____ .   a. **does**   b. **before**   c. **door**

6. Some people will ____ at the store.   a. **happen**   b. **remain**   c. **bring**

7. Use your pencil on this ____ .   a. **table**   b. **money**   c. **paper**

8. This school has one ____ teachers.   a. **four**   b. **hundred** c. **little**

9. Can that cat ____ on the table?   a. **work**   b. **help**   c. **jump**

10. What will ____ if you wear her clothes?   a. **happen**   b. **head**   c. **answer**

E A syllable is a word part that has a vowel sound. Write each lesson word in the correct column on the chart to show how many syllables it has.

| One Syllable | _____ _____ |
| | _____ _____ |

| Two Syllables | _____ _____ _____ |
| | _____ _____ _____ |

F Write a word from the door that rhymes with each word below.

1. some _____   3. brother _____

2. jump _____   4. door _____

mother
more
many
bump
come

Name _____   Date _____

★ High-Frequency Words · Lesson 9

again	brother	door	happen	hundred
jump	paper	remain	some	was

G **Write an answer to each riddle. Use the words in the box above.**

1. I am a form of the verb *to be*. What am I? _____

2. I am something you write on. What am I? _____

3. I mean "once more." What am I? _____

4. I am a son of your parents. What am I? _____

5. I am something you open. What am I? _____

6. I am what a kangaroo does. What am I? _____

H **Read the paragraphs, then answer the questions.**

Someone was at the door.
"Who is it?" called Rob. He went to the door, but no one was there. He did find the paper on the step. Rob put the paper on a table and went back to his work.
Ding dong. It was the bell again. This time Rob did not jump up.
"Why does this happen when I am working?" he asked. "I'll never get one hundred on my test."
"Remain where you are," said his brother. "It's some children. I'll talk to them."

1. Who is at the door when Rob answers it? _____

2. What does Rob find at the door? _____

3. Why doesn't he answer the door again? _____

4. How does he feel when the bell rings again? _____

5. How does his brother help Rob? _____

6. What do you think Rob's brother tells the children? _____

High-Frequency Words · Lesson 9

Name _____ Date _____

★ High-Frequency Words · Lesson 10

any	because	center	father	more
their	two	want	window	write

A Write a word from the box for each picture.

1. **2**
2.
3.
4.

_____ _____ _____ _____

B A syllable is a word part that has a vowel sound. Write each lesson word in the correct column on the chart to show how many syllables it has.

One Syllable	_____ _____ _____
	_____ _____ _____
Two Syllables	_____ _____ _____
	_____ _____ _____

C Write a lesson word for each clue.

1. Write a word that ends in *y*. _____

2. Write a word that sounds like *to*. _____

3. Write a word that has the word *win* in it. _____

4. Write a word that rhymes with *for*. _____

5. Write a word that begins with *wr*. _____

6. Write a word that sounds like *there*. _____

7. Write a word that starts with *be*. _____

8. Write a word that ends in *nt*. _____

9. Write two words that end in *er*. _____

★ High-Frequency Words · Lesson 10

any	because	center	father	more
their	two	want	window	write

D **Read each sentence. Find and circle the word that best fits.**

1. Did you buy ____ paper at the store?   a. **and**   b. **any**   c. **both**

2. Set the dish in the ____ of the table.   a. **center**   b. **circle**   c. **bread**

3. She will ____ a letter to her brother.   a. **ask**   b. **help**   c. **write**

4. Lots of light comes in that ____ .   a. **walk**   b. **window**   c. **month**

5. His ____ buys clothes in the city.   a. **people**   b. **children**   c. **father**

6. Can you find ____ address?   a. **their**   b. **teacher**   c. **they**

7. What do you ____ to put on your bread?   a. **want**   b. **has**   c. **work**

8. I want four ____ pencils for school.   a. **many**   b. **more**   c. **each**

9. The ____ girls are twins.   a. **seven**   b. **one**   c. **two**

10. They need a big house ____ their family is big.   a. **so**   b. **because**   c. **with**

E **Write *yes* or *no* to answer each question.**

1. Does a school have a window?   _____

2. Does a circle have a center?   _____

3. Is eight more than seven?   _____

4. Does a father have children?   _____

5. Does *trio* mean "two"?   _____

F **Write the missing vowels in each word below.**

1. m ___ r ___   2. th ___ ___ r   3. ___ ny   4. tw ___

★ High-Frequency Words · Lesson 10

any	because	center	father	more
their	two	want	window	write

G **Write an answer to each riddle. Use the words in the box above.**

1. I am part of a house. What am I? _____

2. I am the middle. What am I? _____

3. I mean "belonging to them." What am I? _____

4. I am the opposite of *less*. What am I? _____

5. I am a male parent. What am I? _____

6. I am what a pencil does. What am I? _____

H **Read the paragraphs, then answer the questions.**

Bud looked at the window in the Goods' house. It had a crack in the center.

Bud looked at his ball. "This ball doesn't go where I want it to," he said.

Bud talked to his father about the Goods' window.

"You have done that two times," said his father. "You will have to write them a note, and you will have to pay for their new window from your own money."

"It was because of my ball," said Bud. "I won't use it any more."

1. What did Bud do to the window? _____

2. Has Bud done this before? How do you know? _____

3. What do you think Bud will say in his note? _____

4. What else does Bud's father want him to do? _____

5. How do you think Bud's father feels? _____

6. Do you think Bud understands who is to blame? Explain. _____

_____

★ High-Frequency Words · Lesson 11

also	between	draw	either	half
know	point	shoe	think	word

A Write a word from the box for each picture.

1.    2. (circle half shaded)   3.    4. (hand pointing)

_____   _____   _____   _____

B Circle each ending that can be added to the word to make a new word. Write the new word or words.

1. think   *ed*   *s*   *ing*   _____   _____   _____

2. draw   *s*   *ed*   *ing*   _____   _____   _____

3. know   *ing*   *s*   *ed*   _____   _____   _____

4. point   *s*   *ed*   *ing*   _____   _____   _____

C Write a lesson word for each clue.

1. Write a word that begins with *th*. _____

2. Write a word that ends in *nt*. _____

3. Write a word that has the word *or* in it. _____

4. Write a word that begins with *sh*. _____

5. Write a word that rhymes with *calf*. _____

6. Write a word that ends in *er*. _____

7. Write a word that ends in *o*. _____

8. Write a word that has three *e*'s. _____

9. Write two words that end with a vowel and a *w*. _____

★ High-Frequency Words · Lesson 11

| also | between | draw | either | half |
| know | point | shoe | think | word |

D **Read each sentence. Find and circle the word that best fits.**

1. Silas was _____ the two sisters.
   a. **because**   b. **between**   c. **brother**

2. She drank _____ of her milk.
   a. **both**   b. **each**   c. **half**

3. Did _____ of the children get clothes?
   a. **your**   b. **either**   c. **that**

4. Say the _____ before you spell it.
   a. **word**   b. **work**   c. **write**

5. Sandy could not find one _____ .
   a. **shoe**   b. **should**   c. **she**

6. Use the _____ of the pencil to write.
   a. **paper**   b. **light**   c. **point**

7. What do you _____ about this book?
   a. **this**   b. **want**   c. **think**

8. Lucy likes to _____ on light paper.
   a. **walk**   b. **draw**   c. **circle**

9. Do you _____ where our house is?
   a. **know**   b. **bring**   c. **more**

10. Buy bread and _____ some milk.
    a. **ask**   b. **any**   c. **also**

E **Write a word from the bubble that rhymes with each word below.**

1. draw _____   4. word _____

2. point _____   5. half _____

3. think _____   6. either _____

neither could
they laugh
joint
pink saw
bird

F **Circle the correct homophone for each word meaning. (A *homophone* is a word that sounds like another word but has a different meaning and a different spelling.)**

1. to have information   **no**   **know**

2. covering for a foot   **shoo**   **shoe**

★ High-Frequency Words · Lesson 11

also	between	draw	either	half
know	point	shoe	think	word

G **Write *yes* or *no* to answer each question.**

1. Is June between May and July? _____

2. Does a cone have a point? _____

3. Is a shoe for your head? _____

4. Is *two* half of eight? _____

5. Can you draw water from a well? _____

6. Does *also* mean "too"? _____

H **Read the paragraphs, then answer the questions.**

Ali and Cara stopped at a shoe store and looked in the window.

"I think that pair is nice," said Cara. "I also like the red ones."

"Either pair is great," agreed Ali.

They went into the store and had a word with the salesman. He asked Cara to point out the shoes she liked.

"They are between the tan shoes and the boots," she told him.

"I know the ones you mean," said the man. "Both pairs are on sale for half price."

He went to get the shoes, but the store did not have Cara's size.

"Try our other store," said the salesman. "I will draw a map to show you where it is."

1. Where did Ali and Cara stop? _____

2. Why did they go into the store? _____

3. Why did the salesman think Cara could get a good buy? _____

4. Why didn't she buy anything at this store? _____

5. Do you think the salesman was helpful? Explain. _____

6. Do you think Cara will get new shoes? Explain. _____

_____

Name _____   Date _____

begin	country	even	her	large
mother	right	water	would	yellow

A Write a word from the box for each picture.

1.   2.   3.   4.

_____   _____   _____   _____

B Draw a line from each word in the top row to its antonym in the bottom row.
(An *antonym* is a word that has the opposite meaning from another word.)

1. begin   **2.** right   **3.** large   **4.** country   **5.** even   **6.** mother

a. **uneven**   b. **small**   c. **city**   d. **father**   e. **left**   f. **end**

C Write a lesson word for each clue.

1. Write a word that ends in *y*.   _____

2. Write a word that sounds like *write*.   _____

3. Write a word that rhymes with *barge*.   _____

4. Write a word that has *th* in the middle.   _____

5. Write a word that begins with *e*.   _____

6. Write a word that has the word *yell* in it.   _____

7. Write a word that rhymes with *sir*.   _____

8. Write a word that has the word *be* in it.   _____

9. Write two words that begin with *w*.   _____ _____

Name _____ Date _____

★ High-Frequency Words · Lesson 12

begin	country	even	her	large
mother	right	water	would	yellow

D Read each sentence. Find and circle the word that best fits.

1. The teacher told us to circle the ____ answer.   a. **read**   b. **right**   c. **light**

2. We sat at a ____ table.   a. **large**   b. **more**   c. **about**

3. When do the children ____ school?   a. **bring**   b. **begin**   c. **before**

4. Jon used a ____ pencil to draw on the paper.   a. **circle**   b. **letter**   c. **yellow**

5. Yoko is from the ____ of Japan.   a. **city**   b. **country**   c. **center**

6. She ____ like to ask you a question.   a. **could**   b. **should**   c. **would**

7. Will and Connie have an ____ number of points.   a. **even**   b. **each**   c. **eight**

8. Dad put some ____ on the table.   a. **was**   b. **want**   c. **water**

9. Pat calls ____ sister and brother each month.   a. **for**   b. **her**   c. **she**

10. Will your ____ remain with the children?   a. **money**   b. **month**   c. **mother**

E Draw a line from each word in the top row to its synonym in the bottom row. (A *synonym* is a word with almost the same meaning as another word.)

1. mother   2. large   3. right   4. begin   5. country

a. **big**   b. **correct**   c. **nation**   d. **mom**   e. **start**

F Each word below is found in a word in the box at the top of the page. Write the word from the box.

1. at _____   4. moth _____

2. try _____   5. rig _____

3. low _____   6. beg _____

★ High-Frequency Words · Lesson 12

begin	country	even	her	large
mother	right	water	would	yellow

G **Write an answer to each riddle. Use the words in the box above.**

1. I am something you drink. What am I? _____

2. I am a sunny color. What am I? _____

3. I am part of a family. What am I? _____

4. I am the opposite of *odd*. What am I? _____

5. I sound like the word *wood*. What am I? _____

6. I also mean "great." What am I? _____

H **Read the paragraphs, then answer the questions.**

Sam and his mother are going to the country to see her father. They begin their trip right before one o'clock. Sam is feeling sad because his dog, Star, remains at home with his sister. He looks out the window and thinks about Star. His mother talks, but he doesn't listen.

Then she says, "I would like to get to the house by four so we can take a walk with my father before supper. We could even go for a dip in the lake if the water is not too cold."

Sam looks up. By the time they get to the large yellow house, he is thinking about jumping into the water.

1. Why are Sam and his mother going to the country? _____

2. Why is Sam feeling sad? _____

3. How does he show he is sad? _____

4. What does his mother say? _____

5. Do you think his mother knows how Sam feels? Explain. _____

6. What will Sam do when he gets to the house? _____

★ High-Frequency Words · Lesson 13

above	change	earth	finish	friend
here	present	suit	thank	watch

A Write a word from the box for each picture.

1.    2.    3.    4.

_____   _____   _____   _____

B Draw a line from each word in the top row to its synonym in the bottom row. (A *synonym* is a word with almost the same meaning as another word.)

1. above   **2.** friend   **3.** watch   **4.** present   **5.** earth   **6.** change

a. **alter**   b. **gift**   c. **over**   d. **world**   e. **pal**   f. **clock**

C Write a lesson word for each clue.

1. Write a word that begins with *th*. _____

2. Write a word that sounds like *hear*. _____

3. Write a word that ends in *sh*. _____

4. Write a word that begins with *fr*. _____

5. Write a word that rhymes with *boot*. _____

6. Write a word that begins with *pr*. _____

7. Write a word that ends in *th*. _____

8. Write a word that begins with *a*. _____

9. Write two words that have *ch* in them. _____ _____

★ High-Frequency Words · Lesson 13

above	change	earth	finish	friend
here	present	suit	thank	watch

D Read each sentence. Find and circle the word that best fits.

1. Many people are ____ for his talk.   a. **head**   b. **happen**   c. **here**

2. Nina made a ____ on her paper.   a. **change**   b. **draw**   c. **clothes**

3. His father will ____ the children.   a. **with**   b. **watch**   c. **water**

4. Debby asked a ____ to her house.   a. **people**   b. **children**   c. **friend**

5. Can you ____ the work by eight?   a. **light**   b. **finish**   c. **ask**

6. Hank gave me a ____ in yellow paper.   a. **bread**   b. **window**   c. **present**

7. His father had on a new ____ .   a. **suit**   b. **clothes**   c. **circle**

8. The dog dug up the ____ by the house.   a. **earth**   b. **each**   c. **either**

9. The light was ____ the table.   a. **more**   b. **about**   c. **above**

10. Did you ____ her for the shoes?   a. **thank**   b. **think**   c. **this**

E Write a word from the present that rhymes with each word below.

1. friend _____   4. here _____

2. change _____   5. suit _____

3. thank _____

deer   toot
trend   bank
that   range
store

F Draw a line from each word in the top row to its antonym in the bottom row. (An *antonym* is a word that has the opposite meaning from another word.)

1. above   2. here   3. finish   4. change   5. friend

a. **enemy**   b. **preserve**   c. **below**   d. **there**   e. **begin**

★ High-Frequency Words · Lesson 13

above	change	earth	finish	friend
here	present	suit	thank	watch

G **Write *yes* or *no* to answer each question.**

1. Do you thank people for presents?   _____

2. Is the floor above you?   _____

3. Can you buy milk with change?   _____

4. Does a suit have two parts?   _____

5. Is the earth yellow?   _____

6. Do you listen to a friend?   _____

H **Read the clues. Then complete the puzzle with the lesson words.**

ACROSS

4. in a higher place

6. gift

8. make something different

9. express gratitude

10. soil

DOWN

1. complete

2. a timepiece

3. someone you know and like

5. clothes for work

7. in this place

★ High-Frequency Words · Lesson 14

away	business	color	don't	few
interest	mind	none	own	through

A Read the lesson words above. Write a word that fits each shape.

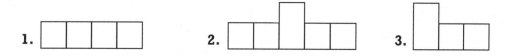

1. ⬜⬜⬜⬜

2. ⬜⬜⬜⬜⬜

3. ⬜⬜⬜

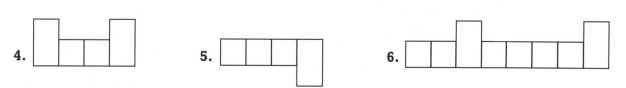

4. ⬜⬜⬜⬜

5. ⬜⬜⬜⬜

6. ⬜⬜⬜⬜⬜⬜⬜

B On another sheet of paper, make a shape for each word you did not use. Write the words below.

1. _____   3. _____

2. _____   4. _____

C Write a lesson word for each clue.

1. Write a word that rhymes with *kind*.   _____

2. Write a word that sounds like *nun*.   _____

3. Write a word that begins with *thr*.   _____

4. Write a word that has the word *way* in it.   _____

5. Write a word that is a contraction.   _____

6. Write a word that has *l* in the middle.   _____

7. Write two words with three syllables.   _____ _____

8. Write two words with three letters.   _____ _____

away	business	color	don't	few
interest	mind	none	own	through

D **Read each sentence. Find and circle the word that best fits.**

1. They will go ____ this month.   a. **above**   b. **away**   c. **about**

2. Do you have any ____ in going out?   a. **interest**   b. **finish**   c. **present**

3. Many people walk ____ the city.   a. **through**   b. **above**   c. **thank**

4. What ____ is your new suit?   a. **center**   b. **clothes**   c. **color**

5. The children ____ listen to their mother.   a. **door**   b. **don't**   c. **want**

6. Her father works at a ____ center.   a. **because**   b. **before**   c. **business**

7. Does your dog ____ you?   a. **mend**   b. **mind**   c. **more**

8. You can either ____ a house or rent it.   a. **draw**   b. **door**   c. **own**

9. A ____ people got on the bus.   a. **few**   b. **none**   c. **half**

10. ____ of the children are in the water.   a. **Large**   b. **Little**   c. **None**

E **Draw a line from each word in the top row to its antonym in the bottom row. (An *antonym* is a word that has the opposite meaning from another word.)**

1. away   2. none   3. don't   4. interest

a. **do**   b. **disinterest**   c. **here**   d. **all**

F **Write *yes* or *no* to answer each question.**

1. Is yellow a dark color? _____   4. Is a store a business? _____

2. Can *through* mean "over"? _____   5. Does *don't* mean "do not"? _____

3. Can interest cost money? _____

★ High-Frequency Words · Lesson 14

away	business	color	don't	few
interest	mind	none	own	through

G Draw a line from each word in the top row to its synonym in the bottom row.
(A *synonym* is a word with almost the same meaning as another word.)

1. few   **2.** color   **3.** mind   **4.** own   **5.** away   **6.** interest

a. **far**   b. **curiosity**   c. **little**   d. **brain**   e. **possess**   f. **hue**

H Read the paragraphs, then answer the questions.

It was the day of the big game. J.T. was upset because his mother was away on business.

"I hope you don't mind too much," she had said before she went. "I *do* have interest in seeing your game. However, when you have your own business, you must work a lot."

But J.T. did mind. His mother had been to so few games, two this month and none the month before.

Even so, J.T. played well and made some big points. When the game was through, he started to go change. Then he saw a large balloon the color of sunshine in the crowd. He began to run. "She must have rushed back!" he said.

1. Why was J.T. upset? _____

2. Why was his mother away? _____

3. Why did she work a lot? _____

4. How did the game go? _____

5. How did J.T. know his mother was there? _____

6. Why do you think his mother rushed back? _____

★ High-Frequency Words · Lesson 15

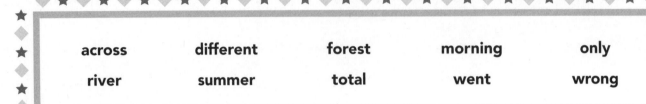

across	different	forest	morning	only
river	summer	total	went	wrong

A Write a word from the box for each picture.

1. _____

2. _____

3. _____

4. $7 + 1 = 8$
_____

B Draw a line from each word in the top row to its synonym in the bottom row.
(A *synonym* is a word with almost the same meaning as another word.)

1. wrong   **2.** forest   **3.** total   **4.** across   **5.** different

a. **unlike**   b. **sum**   c. **over**   d. **incorrect**   e. **woods**

C Write a lesson word for each clue.

1. Write a word that ends in *y*. _____

2. Write a word that rhymes with *bent*. _____

3. Write a word that ends in *st*. _____

4. Write a word that has the word *tot* in it. _____

5. Write a word with two *s*'s. _____

6. Write a word that begins with *wr*. _____

7. Write a word that ends in *ing*. _____

8. Write a word with two *f*'s. _____

9. Write two words ending in *er*. _____ _____

★ High-Frequency Words · Lesson 15

across	different	forest	morning	only
river	summer	total	went	wrong

D Read each sentence. Find and circle the word that best fits.

1. What will you do this ____ ?   a. **happen**   b. **window**   c. **summer**

2. The brothers have ____ suits.   a. **between**   b. **different**   c. **clothes**

3. She was the ____ one in the store.   a. **our**   b. **only**   c. **some**

4. Our house is by the ____ .   a. **remain**   b. **read**   c. **river**

5. He walks to work in the ____ .   a. **morning**   b. **money**   c. **finish**

6. Her answer on the test was ____ .   a. **wrong**   b. **watch**   c. **write**

7. He called to me ____ the river.   a. **half**   b. **begin**   c. **across**

8. What is the ____ for the bill?   a. **total**   b. **talk**   c. **thank**

9. They ____ to school each morning.   a. **where**   b. **with**   c. **went**

10. They walked by tall trees in the ____ .   a. **paper**   b. **forest**   c. **business**

E Each word below is found in a word in the box at the top of the page. Write the word from the box.

1. rent _____   4. for _____

2. we _____   5. sum _____

3. cross _____   6. to _____

F Draw a line from each word in the top row to its antonym in the bottom row. (An *antonym* is a word that has the opposite meaning from another word.)

1. different   2. morning   3. went   4. summer   5. wrong

a. **night**   b. **winter**   c. **right**   d. **same**   e. **came**

★ High-Frequency Words · Lesson 15

across	different	forest	morning	only
river	summer	total	went	wrong

G **Write an answer to each riddle. Use the words in the box above.**

1. I am home to lots of animals. What am I? _____

2. I begin the day. What am I? _____

3. I am a season. What am I? _____

4. I flow over the earth. What am I? _____

5. I can mean "all of something." What am I? _____

6. I am the past tense of "go." What am I? _____

H **Read the paragraphs, then answer the questions.**

This summer my family went away for two weeks. We stayed in a tent by a river. Each morning we swam across the water to the other side.

The tent was only a short walk from a forest with many different trails.

One day we took the wrong path and got lost. It took a long time to find our tent again. But on the way we saw a total of five different animals. Getting lost was okay!

1. When did the family go away? _____

2. Where did the family stay? _____

3. What did they do in the morning? _____

4. How did they get lost? _____

5. Why weren't they upset about getting lost? _____

6. How do you think this family feels about nature? _____

★ High-Frequency Words · Lesson 16

after	best	carry	down	love
now	picture	round	small	winter

A Write a word from the box for each picture.

1.
2.
3.
4.

_____   _____   _____   _____

B A syllable is a word part that has a vowel sound. Write each lesson word in the correct column on the chart to show how many syllables it has.

One Syllable	_____	_____	_____
	_____	_____	_____
Two Syllables	_____	_____	
	_____	_____	

C Write a lesson word for each clue.

1. Write a word that ends in *st*.   _____

2. Write a word that begins with *sm*.   _____

3. Write a word with two *r*'s.   _____

4. Write a word with three letters.   _____

5. Write a word that rhymes with *glove*.   _____

6. Write a word that ends in *nd*.   _____

7. Write a word that begins like *picnic*.   _____

8. Write a word that has the word *do* in it. _____

9. Write two words that end in *er*.   _____   _____

★ High-Frequency Words · Lesson 16

after	best	carry	down	love
now	picture	round	small	winter

D **Read each sentence. Find and circle the word that best fits.**

1. This ____ shows the forest in summer.   a. **business**   b. **picture**   c. **present**

2. Molly wore her ____ clothes to the party.   a. **either**   b. **brother**   c. **best**

3. Come to my house ____ you finish your work.   a. **away**   b. **after**   c. **about**

4. Few birds remain here in ____ .   a. **window**   b. **water**   c. **winter**

5. Abdul will ____ his little brother to the river.   a. **carry**   b. **change**   c. **center**

6. Can you get away right ____?   a. **now**   b. **none**   c. **more**

7. They ____ to be in the country in the morning.   a. **little**   b. **listen**   c. **love**

8. The ____ children had seven cups of milk.   a. **small**   b. **color**   c. **wrong**

9. They went ____ to the river to fish.   a. **door**   b. **down**   c. **don't**

10. The ____ , yellow sun hung over the Earth.   a. **only**   b. **change**   c. **round**

E **Draw a line from each word in the top row to its antonym in the bottom row. (An *antonym* is a word that has the opposite meaning from another word.)**

1. down   2. after   3. now   4. best   5. love   6. winter

a. **hate**   b. **summer**   c. **worst**   d. **up**   e. **before**   f. **then**

F **Write a word from the clown that rhymes with each word below.**

1. best _____   4. round _____

2. down _____   5. small _____

3. now _____

tall   hound
rest   point
mind   clown
shoe   cow

★ High-Frequency Words · Lesson 16

after	best	carry	down	love
now	picture	round	small	winter

G Draw a line from each word on the left to its synonym on the right.
(A *synonym* is a word with almost the same meaning as another word.)

1. carry   a. **immediately**

2. now   b. **little**

3. love   c. **image**

4. small   d. **tote**

5. after   e. **adore**

6. picture   f. **behind**

H Read the paragraph, then answer the questions.

   I love to walk in the forest with my father after a winter snowfall. I
wear my yellow down coat and a wool hat. We carry a small backpack
with water, snacks, and a camera. Now and then, Dad will say, "Wait,
John!" Then he will stop and take a picture. One of his best pictures is
of a red fox. I love how the fox looks against the deep, white snow with
its dark, round eyes looking right at us.

1. Who is telling this story? _____

2. What season is it? _____

3. How do the boy and his father prepare for their walks? _____

4. What does the father like to do? _____

5. Why does the boy like the picture of the fox? _____

6. How do the boy and his father feel about the walks? _____

★ High-Frequency Words · Lesson 17

always	believe	early	guess	laugh
most	off	saw	show	wash

A Write a word from the box for each picture.

   HA-HA

1. _____ 2. _____ 3. _____ 4. _____

B Circle each ending that can be added to the word to make a new word. Write the new word or words.

1. laugh   s   ed   ing   _____ _____ _____

2. wash   ing   ed   es   _____ _____ _____

3. show   s   ing   ed   _____ _____ _____

4. guess   ed   es   ing   _____ _____ _____

C Write a lesson word for each clue.

1. Write a word that has two *f*'s   _____

2. Write a word that ends in *ly*.   _____

3. Write a word that begins with *gu*.   _____

4. Write a word that ends in *st*.   _____

5. Write a word that is the past tense of *see*. _____

6. Write a word that ends in *gh*.   _____

7. Write a word that begins with *al*.   _____

8. Write a word that begins with *be*.   _____

9. Write two words with *sh* in them.   _____ _____

★ High-Frequency Words · Lesson 17

always	believe	early	guess	laugh
most	off	saw	show	wash

D **Read each sentence. Find and circle the word that best fits.**

1. Do you ____ in good luck?   a. **business**   b. **because**   c. **believe**

2. This picture makes people ____ .   a. **laugh**   b. **interest**   c. **best**

3. Turn ____ the light.   a. **off**   b. **one**   c. **point**

4. They ____ Alan last week.   a. **was**   b. **saw**   c. **so**

5. My friend is ____ on time.   a. **half**   b. **few**   c. **always**

6. I will ____ the answer to the question.   a. **total**   b. **guess**   c. **carry**

7. When does the ____ begin?   a. **milk**   b. **show**   c. **circle**

8. The teacher got to school ____ .   a. **early**   b. **even**   c. **earth**

9. He does ____ of his work in the city.   a. **many**   b. **most**   c. **either**

10. Dad will ____ the windows.   a. **walk**   b. **word**   c. **wash**

E **Write *yes* or *no* to answer each question.**

1. Do you laugh at a joke?   _____   4. Does *most* mean "all"?   _____

2. Does *always* mean "forever"?   _____   5. Can you guess someone's age?   _____

3. Is a saw a tool?   _____

F **Each word below is found in a word in the box at the top of the page. Write the word from the box.**

1. how _____   4. way _____

2. ear _____   5. of _____

3. ash _____   6. eve _____

★ High-Frequency Words · Lesson 17

always	believe	early	guess	laugh
most	off	saw	show	wash

G **Write an answer to each riddle. Use the words in the box above.**

1. I am the opposite of *least*. What am I? _____

2. I am a performance. What am I? _____

3. I am what you do in a shower. What am I? _____

4. I am what you do when you have faith. What am I? _____

5. I am what a clown makes you do. What am I? _____

6. I am the opposite of *late*. What am I? _____

H **Read the paragraph, then answer the questions.**

Most of the time Ginger comes when we call her. She always comes when we feed her. She likes to show off her tricks: sit; lie down; shake hands. Ginger is a country dog and she runs in the woods each morning. One day she came home early. We had to laugh when we saw her. What a mess! Ginger had something purple all over her. We had to wash her two times. What happened to her? We can only guess. We believe she ran into a berry bush.

1. Who is Ginger? _____

2. How do you know Ginger likes to eat? _____

3. What are some of her tricks? _____

4. Where does Ginger live? _____

5. Why did the family laugh at Ginger? _____

6. What do you think happened to Ginger? _____

Name _____   Date _____

★ High-Frequency Words · Lesson 18

around	beautiful	build	funny	great
hour	number	office	son	woman

A Write a word from the box for each picture.

1. _____

2. **468**

_____

3. _____

DENTIST

4. _____

B Circle the correct homophone for each word meaning. (A *homophone* is a word that sounds like another word but has a different meaning and a different spelling.)

1. big	grate	great
2. the male child of parents	sun	son
3. 60 minutes	hour	our

C Write a lesson word for each clue.

1. Write a word that ends in *er*.   _____

2. Write a word with three letters.   _____

3. Write a word with the word *man* in it.   _____

4. Write a word that ends in *nd*.   _____

5. Write a word with three syllables.   _____

6. Write a word that begins with *gr*.   _____

7. Write a word with a silent *h*.   _____

8. Write a word that ends in *ld*.   _____

9. Write two words with double letters.   _____ _____

★ High-Frequency Words · Lesson 18

around	beautiful	build	funny	great
hour	number	office	son	woman

D Read each sentence. Find and circle the word that best fits.

1. Mr. Gelb spoke to his small ____ .   a. **her**   b. **father**   c. **son**

2. They must be at school in one ____ .   a. **hour**   b. **half**   c. **few**

3. Mother's new suit was ____ .   a. **best**   b. **beautiful**   c. **color**

4. He was so ____ that we were all laughing.   a. **funny**   b. **early**   c. **away**

5. The ____ at the store showed us some clothes.   a. **children**   b. **brother**   c. **woman**

6. Most people said the show was ____ .   a. **change**   b. **between**   c. **great**

7. Amy called her friend's ____ .   a. **number**   b. **address**   c. **picture**

8. We ____ to visit our father's office.   a. **think**   b. **love**   c. **been**

9. Mom likes to carry ____ our picture.   a. **above**   b. **also**   c. **around**

10. I believe they will ____ a new house here.   a. **total**   b. **build**   c. **wash**

E Draw a line from each word in the top row to its synonym in the bottom row.
(A *synonym* is a word with almost the same meaning as another word.)

1. funny   2. beautiful   3. woman   4. great   5. build   6. office

a. **construct**   b. **large**   c. **amusing**   d. **workplace**   e. **pretty**   f. **lady**

F Write a word from the building that rhymes with each word below.

1. son   _____

2. funny   _____

3. great   _____

fun how
sound
late sunny

★ High-Frequency Words · Lesson 18

around	beautiful	build	funny	great
hour	number	office	son	woman

G Draw a line from each word in the top row to its antonym in the bottom row. (An *antonym* is a word that has the opposite meaning from another word.)

1. woman   2. funny   3. beautiful   4. son   5. build   6. great

a. small   b. man   c. sad   d. destroy   e. ugly   f. daughter

H Read the clues. Then complete the puzzle with the lesson words.

1. very good
2. lovely
3. female
4. in a circle
5. silly
6. boy child
7. unit of time
8. place to work
9. make something
10. word that tells how many

1. ☐ R ☐ ☐ ☐
2. ☐ E ☐ ☐ ☐ ☐ ☐ ☐
3. ☐ ☐ ☐ A ☐
4. ☐ ☐ ☐ ☐ ☐ D
5. ☐ F ☐ ☐ ☐ ☐
6. ☐ O ☐
7. ☐ ☐ ☐ R
8. ☐ ☐ F ☐ ☐ ☐
9. ☐ U ☐ ☐ ☐
10. N ☐ ☐ ☐ ☐ ☐

★ High-Frequency Words · Lesson 19

company	every	high	learn	never
please	reason	soon	true	year

A Read the lesson words above. Write a word that fits each shape.

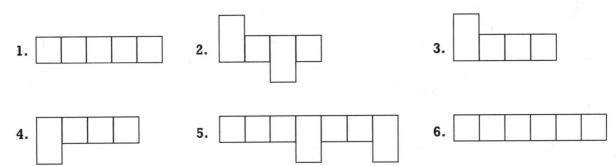

1.

2.

3.

4.

5.

6.

B On another sheet of paper, make a shape for each word you did not use. Write the words below.

1. _____   3. _____

2. _____   4. _____

C Write a lesson word for each clue.

1. Write a word that begins with *tr*. _____

2. Write a word that ends in *er*. _____

3. Write a word that begins with *pl*. _____

4. Write a word with double *o's*. _____

5. Write a word that ends in *gh*. _____

6. Write a word that rhymes with *dear*. _____

7. Write a word that ends in *rn*. _____

8. Write a word with the word *son* in it. _____

9. Write two words that end in *y*. _____

★ High-Frequency Words · Lesson 19

company	every	high	learn	never
please	reason	soon	true	year

D **Read each sentence. Find and circle the word that best fits.**

1. She works for a paper ____ .   a. **country**   b. **company**   c. **money**

2. The answer was either ____ or false.   a. **true**   b. **two**   c. **total**

3. In what ____ were you born?   a. **year**   b. **office**   c. **window**

4. The map shows ____ city in the state.   a. **early**   b. **every**   c. **eight**

5. Will you ____ get up from the table?   a. **finish**   b. **remain**   c. **please**

6. The milk was on a ____ shelf.   a. **half**   b. **hour**   c. **high**

7. Our teacher wants us to ____ .   a. **build**   b. **learn**   c. **guess**

8. He had a good ____ for being late.   a. **reason**   b. **many**   c. **interest**

9. That funny show will ____ be on TV.   a. **most**   b. **begin**   c. **soon**

10. You ____ listen to me!   a. **again**   b. **never**   c. **because**

E **Each word below is found in a word in the box at the top of the page. Write the word from the box.**

1. hi _____   2. lease _____   3. yea _____

4. earn _____   5. any _____   6. very _____

F **A syllable is a word part that has a vowel sound. Write lesson words in the correct column on the chart to show how many syllables they have.**

Two Syllables	_____ _____
Three Syllables	_____ _____

★ High-Frequency Words · Lesson 19

company	every	high	learn	never
please	reason	soon	true	year

G **Write an answer to each riddle. Use the words in the box above.**

1. I am a business. What am I? _____

2. I am 12 months. What am I? _____

3. I am what you do in school. What am I? _____

4. I mean "not ever." What am I? _____

5. I am the opposite of *low*. What am I? _____

6. I am a polite word. What am I? _____

H **Read the paragraphs, then answer the questions.**

"Would you please change into your clothes?' I said to my brother Salim. "We are having company."

My brother was reading on the top bunk of our beds. He looked down from his high reading place. "Soon," he said. "I want to finish this book."

"He never listens," I said to Mom. "Every time I ask, he puts me off."

It was true. My brother always had a reason for not doing what I asked. But this year, Salim did learn something. When his friends showed up for a surprise party, he was still in bed in his pj's! It was so funny! I laughed most of all.

1. Who is telling this story? _____

2. Where was Salim? _____

3. What was he asked to do? _____

4. Why didn't Salim do as he was asked? _____

5. What did Salim learn? _____

6. How do you think Salim felt when everyone laughed at him? _____

_____

★ High-Frequency Words · Lesson 20

able	better	cover	doesn't	follow
hurt	long	return	thought	visit

A **Write a word from the box for each picture.**

1. _____ 2. _____ 3. _____ 4. _____

B **Draw a line from each word in the top row to its antonym in the bottom row. (An *antonym* is a word that has the opposite meaning from another word.)**

1. cover   **2.** long   **3.** follow   **4.** able   **5.** doesn't   **6.** better

a. **does**   b. **uncover**   c. **worse**   d. **short**   e. **unable**   f. **lead**

C **Write a lesson word for each clue.**

1. Write a word that begins with *th*. _____

2. Write a word that ends in *ng*. _____

3. Write a word that rhymes with *table*. _____

4. Write a word that ends in *rt*. _____

5. Write a word that has two *l*'s. _____

6. Write a word that is a contraction. _____

7. Write a word that begins with *re*. _____

8. Write a word that has the word *it* in it. _____

9. Write two words that end in *er*. _____ _____

★ High-Frequency Words · Lesson 20

able	better	cover	doesn't	follow
hurt	long	return	thought	visit

D **Read each sentence. Find and circle the word that best fits.**

1. My sister went to ____ a friend.   a. **visit**   b. **with**   c. **work**

2. I want to be a ____ reader.   a. **best**   b. **better**   c. **believe**

3. Did that dog ____ me home?   a. **return**   b. **follow**   c. **ask**

4. We thought the show was too ____ .   a. **round**   b. **away**   c. **long**

5. He was ____ to draw a great picture.   a. **able**   b. **after**   c. **above**

6. Where is the ____ for this box?   a. **door**   b. **window**   c. **cover**

7. Did you ____ your hand when you fell?   a. **hurt**   b. **hour**   c. **help**

8. Dad will ____ from the office soon.   a. **remain**   b. **return**   c. **reason**

9. Jake ____ know our address.   a. **happen**   b. **is**   c. **doesn't**

10. I ____ her clothes were beautiful.   a. **thought**   b. **through**   c. **thank**

E **Circle each ending that can be added to the word to make a new word. Write the new word or words.**

1. visit   *ed*   *s*   *ing*   _____   _____   _____

2. return   *s*   *ed*   *ing*   _____   _____   _____

3. follow   *s*   *ed*   *ing*   _____   _____   _____

F **Write *yes* or *no* to answer each question.**

1. Can you cover a jar? _____   4. Can you see a thought? _____

2. Can you return a book? _____   5. Can you follow a path? _____

3. Can you hurt a stone? _____

★ High-Frequency Words · Lesson 20

able	better	cover	doesn't	follow
hurt	long	return	thought	visit

G **Write an answer to each riddle. Use the words in the box above.**

1. I am a form of the word *good*. What am I? _____

2. I can be found on a bed. What am I? _____

3. I mean "does not." What am I? _____

4. I am what guests do. What am I? _____

5. I can mean "to wish for." What am I? _____

6. I am what an injury does. What am I? _____

H **Read the paragraphs, then answer the questions.**

A friend came to visit my big sister, Ella.

"How long will Lin stay?" I asked. "How many days?"

My sister was hurt by my questions. She thought I was rude.

"Cover your mouth, Doug" she said. "You had better be nice to Lin, or I'll never speak to you again."

I did my best and was able to stay out of their way. But after a week, Ella came to me and said, "I wish Lin didn't follow me around all the time. I can't wait for her to return home!"

I had to laugh. "It doesn't pay to listen to your big sister," I said. "You are hard to please."

1. Who came to visit? _____

2. Why was Ella hurt? _____

3. What did Ella tell Doug? _____

4. What did Doug do after that? _____

5. Why did Ella change her mind? _____

6. Why did Doug laugh at Ella? _____

★ High-Frequency Words · Lesson 21

another	government	live	minute	once
remember	smile	thing	wear	which

A Write a word from the box for each picture.

1.  _____

2. [picture] _____

B A syllable is a word part that has a vowel sound. Write each lesson word in the correct column on the chart to show how many syllables it has.

One Syllable	_____	_____	_____
	_____	_____	_____
Two Syllables	_____		
Three Syllables	_____	_____	_____

C Write a lesson word for each clue.

1. Write a word that begins with *th*.   _____

2. Write a word that begins with *wh*.   _____

3. Write a word that ends with the suffix *ment*.   _____

4. Write a word that begins with *sm*.   _____

5. Write a word that has the word *nut* in it.   _____

6. Write a word that begins like *love*.   _____

7. Write a word that rhymes with *fair*.   _____

8. Write a word that has the word *on* in it.   _____

9. Write two words that end in *er*.   _____ _____

★ High-Frequency Words · Lesson 21

another	government	live	minute	once
remember	smile	thing	wear	which

D **Read each sentence. Find and circle the word that best fits.**

1. What will you ____ to school?   a. **follow**   b. **learn**   c. **wear**

2. We ____ at this address.   a. **live**   b. **little**   c. **long**

3. Pepe has a beautiful ____ .   a. **summer**   b. **smile**   c. **through**

4. Dad wants to buy ____ suit.   a. **able**   b. **about**   c. **another**

5. The mail comes ____ a day.   a. **few**   b. **soon**   c. **once**

6. Please don't be a ____ late.   a. **minute**   b. **number**   c. **center**

7. What do you ____ about last summer?   a. **remain**   b. **return**   c. **remember**

8. ____ one is your picture?   a. **Which**   b. **When**   c. **Why**

9. What is that ____ on the door?   a. **reason**   b. **thing**   c. **think**

10. He is the new head of our ____ .   a. **forest**   b. **government**   c. **visit**

E **Circle the correct homophone for each word meaning. (A *homophone* is a word that sounds like another word but has a different meaning and a different spelling.)**

1. put on clothes   where   wear

2. what one   which   witch

F **Write a word from the bear that rhymes with each word below.**

1. live _____   5. wear _____

2. once _____   6. which _____

3. smile _____   7. remember _____

4. thing _____   8. another _____

bear
best
ring
pile
dunce
hurt
mother
September
itch
give

★ High-Frequency Words · Lesson 21

another	government	live	minute	once
remember	smile	thing	wear	which

G **Write an answer to each riddle. Use the words from the box above.**

1. I can be spelled with a long or short *i*. What am I? _____

2. I am part of an hour. What am I? _____

3. I am the opposite of *forget*. What am I? _____

4. I mean "one time." What am I? _____

5. I am what you do when you are happy. What am I? _____

6. I am how a country is run. What am I? _____

H **Read the paragraphs, then answer the questions.**

We talked about jobs today. Mark once visited Washington, D. C., and remembers it well. Now he wants to work for the government. Sally wants to be a model and wear beautiful clothes. Another friend wants to be on TV and make people smile at his jokes.

I don't know what I want to do, but one thing I do know is this: I want to live near my job so I can get to it in a minute. Then I can sleep late, which is what I like to do best!

1. What is the topic of this story? _____

2. Why does Mark want to work for the government? _____

3. Why does Sally want to be a model? _____

4. What does the other friend want to do? _____

5. Why does the person telling the story want to live near his or her job? _____

_____

6. Do you think this person is serious about what he or she said? Why or why not?

_____

Name _____   Date _____

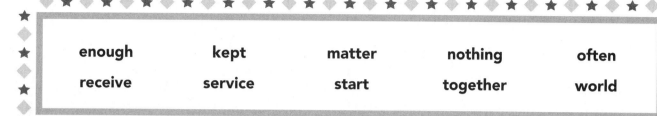

★ High-Frequency Words · Lesson 22

enough	kept	matter	nothing	often
receive	service	start	together	world

A   **Write a word from the box for each picture.**

→ 

1. _____

2. 

    _____

B   **Draw a line from each word in the top row to its antonym in the bottom row.**
(An *antonym* is a word that has the opposite meaning from another word.)

1. together   **2.** nothing   **3.** receive   **4.** often   **5.** start   **6.** enough

a. **rarely**   b. **lacking**   c. **apart**   d. **finish**   e. **everything**   f. **give**

C   **Write a lesson word for each clue.**

1. Write a word that begins with *st*.   _____

2. Write a word that is the past tense of *keep*.   _____

3. Write a word that ends in *ing*.   _____

4. Write a word that has the word *ten* in it.   _____

5. Write a word that rhymes with *believe*.   _____

6. Write a word that ends in *gh*.   _____

7. Write a word that has the word *ice* in it.   _____

8. Write a word that ends in *ld*.   _____

9. Write two words that end in *er*.   _____   _____

★ High-Frequency Words · Lesson 22

enough	kept	matter	nothing	often
receive	service	start	together	world

D **Read each sentence. Find and circle the word that best fits.**

1. We went to school _____ .   a. **remember**   b. **together**   c. **center**

2. The _____ is a large place.   a. **world**   b. **watch**   c. **morning**

3. The _____ at the diner was great.   a. **circle**   b. **service**   c. **number**

4. They _____ went to the city.   a. **off**   b. **own**   c. **often**

5. Mom wanted to get an early _____ .   a. **away**   b. **start**   c. **before**

6. Did you have _____ bread?   a. **enough**   b. **high**   c. **another**

7. What is the _____ with these children? a. **different** b. **matter**   c. **minute**

8. You will _____ their pictures soon. a. **receive**   b. **reason**   c. **remain**

9. There was _____ on the table.   a. **between**   b. **nothing**   c. **together**

10. He _____ his change in a box.   a. **kept**   b. **said**   c. **hurt**

E **Each word below is found in a word in the box at the top of the page. Write the word from the box.**

1. thing _____   4. or _____

2. ugh _____   5. art _____

3. mat _____   6. get _____

F **The vowels _e_ and _o_ are missing from the words below. Add the missing vowels.**

1. ___ n ___ ugh   5. matt ___ r

2. w ___ rld   6. k ___ pt

3. t ___ g ___ th ___ r   7. n ___ thing

4. r ___ c ___ iv ___   8. ___ ft ___ n

★ High-Frequency Words · Lesson 22

enough	kept	matter	nothing	often
receive	service	start	together	world

G Draw a line from each word in the top row to its synonym in the bottom row. (A *synonym* is a word with almost the same meaning as another word.)

1. receive   **2.** kept   **3.** start   **4.** nothing   **5.** often   **6.** service

a. **saved**   b. **military**   c. **zero**   d. **get**   e. **begin**   f. **frequently**

H Read the paragraphs, then answer the questions.

"This car needs service," said Dad. Our car often did because it was old. This time it would not start. Dad kept trying, but no matter what he did, nothing happened.

"It's not getting enough gas," he said.

Just then Tyrone came by. "There is no gas," he pointed out. "The arrow is on empty."

Dad does not always receive bad news well, but this time he laughed. "What in the world? Oh, now I remember! I was going to get some."

Then he and Tyrone went off together to get gas.

1. Why does Dad think the car needs service? _____

2. What does Dad think the problem is? _____

3. How does Tyrone know what the matter is? _____

4. How does Dad usually take bad news? _____

5. Why does Dad take this news well? _____

6. Why do you think Dad forgot to get gas? _____

Name _____ Date _____

★ High-Frequency Words · Lesson 23

except	first	over	pretty	second
sure	today	were	yesterday	young

A Write a word from the box for each picture.

1.  _____

2.  _____

B Write a word from the clover that rhymes with each word below.

1. were _____

2. young _____

3. first _____

4. pretty _____

5. over _____

6. sure _____

lure   clover   lung

worst   love

soon   fur   witty

C Write a lesson word for each clue.

1. Write a word that begins with *pr*. _____

2. Write a word that ends in *ng*. _____

3. Write a word that has the word *to* in it. _____

4. Write a word that begins with *ex*. _____

5. Write a word that is the opposite of *weren't*. _____

6. Write a word that ends in *nd*. _____

7. Write a word that begins with a sound like *sh*. _____

8. Write a word that ends in *er*. _____

9. Write two words with *st* in them. _____ _____

★ High-Frequency Words · Lesson 23

except	first	over	pretty	second
sure	today	were	yesterday	young

D **Read each sentence. Find and circle the word that best fits.**

1. Are you ____ that hat will fit?   a. **once**   b. **wear**   c. **sure**

2. All the children ____ Tony are here.   a. **except**   b. **enough**   c. **either**

3. We ____ in a beautiful forest.   a. **kept**   b. **were**   c. **would**

4. She was the ____ one in line.   a. **most**   b. **which**   c. **first**

5. The story hour was ____ too soon.   a. **long**   b. **once**   c. **over**

6. The woman took her ____ son for a walk. a. **live**   b. **young**   c. **carry**

7. Do you remember what we did ____ ?   a. **yesterday** b. **summer** c. **after**

8. This is her ____ visit this year.   a. **minute**   b. **eight**   c. **second**

9. The light in the forest was a ____ color. a. **pretty** b. **paper**   c. **large**

10. We hope to receive your letter ____ .   a. **true**   b. **today**   c. **total**

E **Draw a line from each word in the top row to its antonym in the bottom row. (An *antonym* is a word that has the opposite meaning from another word.)**

1. over   2. pretty   3. first   4. today   5. young   6. sure

a. **yesterday**   b. **old**   c. **under**   d. **unsure**   e. **ugly**   f. **last**

F **Write *yes* or *no* to answer each question.**

1. Is a baby young? _____   4. Is first at the end? _____

2. Does a bridge go over? _____   5. Can second be a base? _____

3. Is today in the future? _____   6. Does *sure* mean "certain"? _____

★ High-Frequency Words · Lesson 23

except	first	over	pretty	second
sure	today	were	yesterday	young

G **Write an answer to each riddle. Use the words in the box above.**

1. I am used to describe flowers. What am I? _____

2. There are 60 of me in a minute. What am I? _____

3. I tell about the past. What am I? _____

4. I am after kindergarten in school. What am I? _____

5. I am used to describe children. What am I? _____

6. I tell about the present. What am I? _____

H **Read the clues. Then complete the puzzle with the lesson words.**

1. not fully grown

2. coming before others

3. other than

4. the present day

5. the day before

6. the past tense of *are* in the verb "to be"

7. above

8. pleasing or attractive

9. number two in an order

10. without a doubt

1. ☐ ☐ ☐ ☐ G
2. ☐ ☐ R ☐ ☐
3. ☐ E ☐ ☐ ☐ ☐
4. ☐ ☐ ☐ A ☐
5. ☐ ☐ ☐ ☐ T ☐ ☐ ☐ ☐
6. W ☐ ☐ ☐
7. O ☐ ☐
8. ☐ R ☐ ☐ ☐ ☐
9. ☐ ☐ ☐ ☐ ☐ D
10. S ☐ ☐ ☐

★ High-Frequency Words · Lesson 24

among	brought	might	myself	next
those	tomorrow	until	very	won't

A Read the lesson words above. Write a word that fits each shape.

1.

2.

3.

4.

5.

6.

B On another sheet of paper, make a shape for each word you did not use. Write the words below.

1. _____   3. _____

2. _____   4. _____

C Write a lesson word for each clue.

1. Write a word that ends in *xt*.   _____

2. Write a word that begins with *th*.   _____

3. Write a word that is a contraction.   _____

4. Write a word that ends in *y*.   _____

5. Write a word that has the word *to* in it. _____

6. Write a word that ends in *lf*.   _____

7. Write a word that ends in *ng*.   _____

8. Write a word that begins with *un*.   _____

9. Write two words that ends in *ght*.   _____ _____

Name _____ Date _____

★ High-Frequency Words · Lesson 24

| among | brought | might | myself | next |
| those | tomorrow | until | very | won't |

D Read each sentence. Find and circle the word that best fits.

1. Who is ____ in line? a. **next** b. **finish** c. **able**

2. The flowers are ____ pretty. a. **were** b. **very** c. **best**

3. You are ____ friends here. a. **among** b. **away** c. **matter**

4. I hope it ____ rain today. a. **want** b. **wear** c. **won't**

5. The first day of school is ____ . a. **together** b. **thought** c. **tomorrow**

6. We laughed ____ we were sick. a. **often** b. **until** c. **over**

7. She ____ get a job in government. a. **mind** b. **more** c. **might**

8. Will ____ who are new please stand? a. **thank** b. **those** c. **think**

9. I asked ____ what to do next. a. **either** b. **guess** c. **myself**

10. He ____ a letter from the company. a. **brought** b. **better** c. **bread**

E Each word below is found in a word in the box. Write the word from the box.

1. my _____ 3. row _____

2. hose _____ 4. am _____

F Write a word from the rose bush that rhymes with each word below.

1. next _____ 5. very _____

2. might _____ 6. tomorrow _____

3. brought _____

4. those _____

borrow berry sorry text bees light rose thought

High-Frequency Words · Lesson 24

★ High-Frequency Words · Lesson 24

among	brought	might	myself	next
those	tomorrow	until	very	won't

G **Write *yes* or *no* to answer each question.**

1. Is tomorrow after today? _____

2. Does *won't* stand for *will not*? _____

3. Does *next* come before *first*? _____

4. Is *brought* the past tense of *bring*? _____

5. Does *among* mean *between*? _____

6. Is *myself* a form of *me*? _____

H **Read the paragraphs, then answer the questions.**

I was among the students who brought things to sell at the fair today. Our team has done a very good job this year. Now we want to help those who will play next year. We want to be sure they have enough money for bats and balls. We won't know how well we did until tomorrow, when the fair is over. I, myself, might make more cupcakes to sell tomorrow.

I think I remember how to make them.

1. What did the student do? _____

2. Why did the student do this? _____

3. What sport does the team play? _____

4. When will the students know if they made enough money? _____

5. How will this student try to help meet the goal? _____

6. Where do you think the fair took place? _____

Answers

LESSON 1

Page 6: A. 1. has 2. answer 3. this 4. is 5. your 6. sister **B.** 1.–4. by, find, school, what **C.** 1. school 2. this 3. by 4. what 5. your 6. find 7. has 8. is 9. answer, sister **Page 7: D.** 1. b 2. a 3. b 4. c 5. c 6. a 7. b 8. a 9. c 10. b **E.** 1. e 2. f 3. b 4. c 5. d 6. a **F.** 1. is 2. has 3. find **Page 8: G.** 1. yes 2. yes 3. yes 4. no 5. yes **H. Across:** 1. what 3. school 6. sister 9. your 10. find; **Down:** 2. answer 4. has 5. by 7. is 8. this

LESSON 2

Page 9: A. 1. house 2. letter 3. eight **B.** 1. why 2. said 3. been 4. on 5. new 6. the 7. call **C.** 1. why 2. been 3. new 4. said 5. eight 6. on 7. house, the 8. call, letter **Page 10: D.** 1. b 2. a 3. c 4. b 5. b 6. c 7. c 8. a 9. b 10. c **E.** 1. new 2. been **F.** 1. red 2. better 3. hi 4. date 5. mouse 6. fall **Page 11: G.** 1. eight 2. said 3. house 4. why 5. letter 6. call **H.** 1. Lee 2. eight 3. at the house 4. She called Lee. 5. She can read them. 6. Answers will vary.

LESSON 3

Page 12: A. 1. pencil 2. circle 3. family 4. talk **B.** 1. and 2. when 3. use 4. she 5. both 6. go **C.** 1. family 2. pencil 3. when 4. she 5. circle 6. talk 7. and, use 8. both, go **Page 13: D.** 1. c 2. b 3. c 4. a 5. b 6. c 7. a 8. b 9. c 10. b **E.** 1. hand 2. so 3. hen 4. walk 5. he **F.** 1. yes 2. no 3. yes 4. yes **Page 14: G.** 1. she 2. pencil 3. and 4. circle 5. family 6. talk **H.** 1. the Tell family 2. Paul 3. about five 4. Jill 5. a new pencil 6. Answers will vary.

LESSON 4

Page 15: A. 1. city 2. read 3. month **B.** 1. teacher 2. have 3. are 4. with 5. help 6. for 7. do **C.** 1. teacher 2. do 3. city 4. are 5. read 6. for 7. have, help 8. month, with **Page 16: D.** 1. b 2. a 3. a 4. b 5. c 6. b 7. a 8. b 9. b 10. c **E.** 1. are 2. do 3. help **F.** 1. circle 2. form 3. mother 4. reed 5. wit 6. tea **Page 17: G.** 1. e 2. f 3. c 4. a 5. b 6. d **H.** 1. lots of books 2. Jen 3. She teaches her to read. 4. She might not be in school yet. 5. Answers will vary. 6. She is positive, supportive of Sue.

LESSON 5

Page 18: A. 1. money 2. light 3. store **B.** 1. who 2. our 3. could 4. his 5. each 6. they 7. that **C.** 1. could 2. his 3. store 4. money 5. who 6. light 7. each, our, 8. that, they **Page 19: D.** 1. c 2. a 3. b 4. b 5. c 6. b 7. c 8. c 9. b 10. c **E.** 1. d 2. e 3. f 4. b 5. c 6. a **F.** 1. yes 2. yes 3. no 4. yes **Page 20: G.** 1. money 2. that 3. they 4. store 5. light 6. who **H.** 1. He works in his dad's store. 2. He likes it. 3. his dad 4. in the city 5. early in the morning 6. He helps sell things.

LESSON 6

Page 21: A. 1. question 2. four 3. clothes 4. people **B. One Syllable:** ask, clothes, does, four, so, where; **Two Syllables:** before, many, people, question **C.** 1. many 2. ask 3. where 4. people 5. so 6. question 7. does 8. clothes 9. before, four **Page 22: D.** 1. a 2. c 3. c 4. b 5. c 6. b 7. a 8. c 9. a 10. c **E.** 1. care 2. steeple 3. hose 4. mask 5. more 6. go **F.** 1. c 2. d 3. a 4. b **Page 23: G.** 1. many 2. ask 3. where 4. before 5. four 6. clothes **H.** 1. his clothes 2. Ruth 3. Mom 4. She wants Al to find his clothes and go to school. 5. Possible: He doesn't want to go to school. 6. Answers will vary.

LESSON 7

Page 24: A. 1. table 2. one 3. head 4. address **B.** 1. walks, walked 2. worker, working, worked 3. buys, buying 4. comes **C.** 1. head 2. work 3. one 4. should 5. walk 6. buy 7. address 8. come 9. little, table **Page 25: D.** 1. b 2. c 3. b 4. b 5. a 6. a 7. c 8. c 9. b 10. a **E.** 1. c 2. e 3. d 4. f 5. b 6. a **F.** 1. address 2. one 3. table 4. walk **Page 26: G.** 1. yes 2. no 3. yes 4. yes 5. yes 6. no **H.** 1. near Ann's house 2. Lisa 3. to buy new clothes 4. hat 5. Answers will vary. Possible: Yes because there are many to choose from 6. Answers will vary. Possible: tops

LESSON 8

Page 27: A. 1. seven 2. bread 3. milk 4. children **B. One Syllable:** bread, bring, from, goes, milk, of; **Two Syllables:** about, children, listen, seven **C.** 1. from 2. milk 3. children 4. goes 5. about 6. seven 7. of 8. listen 9. bring, bread **Page 28: D.** 1. c 2. b 3. c 4. b 5. a 6. a 7. c 8. b 9. c 10. a **E.** 1. yes 2. yes 3. no 4. yes 5. yes 6. no **F.** 1. bring 2. goes 3. listen **Page 29: G.** 1. milk 2. listen 3. seven 4. goes 5. bread 6. children **H.** 1. from 2. goes 3. bread 4. children 5. listen 6. of 7. milk 8. seven 9. about 10. bring

LESSON 9

Page 30: A. 1. hundred 2. paper 3. door 4. jump **B.** 1. papered, papering, papers 2. happened, happens, happening 3. remaining, remains, remained 4. jumps, jumped, jumping **C.** 1. jump 2. some 3. brother 4. again 5. was 6. paper or happen 7. remain 8. door 9. happen, hundred **Page 31: D.** 1. b 2. a 3. c 4. a 5. c 6. b 7. c 8. b 9. c 10. a **E. One Syllable:** door, jump, some, was; **Two Syllables:** again, brother, happen, hundred, paper, remain **F.** 1. come 2. bump 3. mother 4. more **Page 32: G.** 1. was 2. paper 3. again 4. brother 5. door 6. jump **H.** 1. no one 2. the paper 3. He is studying for a test. 4. He is annoyed. 5. He answers the door. 6. Answers will vary. Possible: He will tell them to go away and not ring the bell again.

LESSON 10

Page 33: A. 1. two 2. window 3. father 4. write **B.** One Syllable: more, their, two, want, write; Two Syllables: because, center, father, window, any **C.** 1. any 2. two 3. window 4. more 5. write 6. their 7. because 8. want 9. center, father **Page 34: D.** 1. b 2. a 3. c 4. b 5. c 6. a 7. a 8. b 9. c 10. b **E.** 1. yes 2. yes 3. yes 4. yes 5. no **F.** 1. more 2. their 3. any 4. two

Page 35: G. 1. window 2. center 3. their 4. more 5. father 6. write **H.** 1. He cracked it. 2. Yes, his father says he has done it two times. 3. Answers will vary. Possible: He might say he is sorry. 4. pay for the window 5. Answers will vary. Possible: He is annoyed with Bud and wants to teach him a lesson. 6. Answers will vary. Possible: No, because he blames it on the ball, not himself.

LESSON 11

Page 36: A. 1. shoe 2. half 3. draw 4. point **B.** 1. thinks, thinking 2. draws, drawing 3. knowing, knows 4. points, pointed, pointing **C.** 1. think 2. point 3. word 4. shoe 5. half 6. either 7. also 8. between 9. draw, know **Page 37: D.** 1. b 2. c 3. b 4. a 5. a 6. c 7. c 8. b 9. a 10. c **E.** 1. saw 2. joint 3. pink 4. bird 5. laugh 6. neither **F.** 1. know 2. shoe **Page 38: G.** 1. yes 2. yes 3. no 4. no 5. yes 6. yes **H.** 1. at a shoe store window 2. They saw shoes they liked. 3. The shoes were on sale for half price. 4. The store didn't have Cara's size. 5. Answers will vary. Possible: Yes, he drew a map so they could go to the other store. 6. Answers will vary. Possible: They will find shoes that fit at the other store.

LESSON 12

Page 39: A. 1. water 2. yellow 3. right 4. mother **B.** 1. f 2. e 3. b 4. c 5. a 6. d **C.** 1. country 2. right 3. large 4. mother 5. even 6. yellow 7. her 8. begin 9. would, water **Page 40: D.** 1. b 2. a 3. b 4. c 5. b 6. c 7. a 8. c 9. b 10. c **E.** 1. d 2. a 3. b 4. e 5. c **F.** 1. water 2. country 3. yellow 4. mother 5. right 6. begin **Page 41: G.** 1. water 2. yellow 3. mother 4. even 5. would 6. large **H.** 1. to see his grandfather 2. His dog is still at home. 3. He looks out the window and doesn't pay attention to his mother. 4. She mentions taking a walk and maybe going for a dip. 5. Answers will vary. Possible: Yes, because she mentions going into the lake. 6. Possible: He will go for a walk and a swim.

LESSON 13

Page 42: A. 1. present 2. watch 3. earth 4. suit **B.** 1. c 2. e 3. f 4. b 5. d 6. a **C.** 1. thank 2. here 3. finish 4. friend 5. suit 6. present 7. earth 8. above 9. change, watch **Page 43: D.** 1. c 2. a 3. b 4. c 5. b 6. c 7. a 8. a 9. c 10. a **E.** 1. trend 2. range 3. bank 4. deer 5. toot **F.** 1. c 2. d 3. e 4. b 5. a **Page 44: G.** 1. yes 2. no 3. yes 4. yes 5. no 6. yes **H.** Across: 1. above 6. present 8. change 9. thank 10. earth; Down: 1. finish 2. watch 3. friend 5. suit 7. here

LESSON 14

Page 45: A. 1. none 2. color 3. few 4. don't 5. away 6. interest **B.** 1.–4. business, mind, own, through **C.** 1. mind 2. none 3. through 4. away 5. don't 6. color 7. business, interest 8. few, own **Page 46: D.** 1. b 2. a 3. a 4. c 5. b 6. c 7. b 8. c 9. a 10. c **E.** 1. c 2. d 3. a 4. b **F.** 1. no 2. yes 3. yes 4. yes 5. yes **Page 47: G.** 1. c 2. f 3. d 4. e 5. a 6. b **H.** 1. His mother wasn't coming to the game. 2. She was on a business trip. 3. She owned her own business. 4. It went well. 5. He saw the balloon. 6. She knew that J.T. was upset.

LESSON 15

Page 48: A. 1. wrong 2. river 3. forest 4. total **B.** 1. d 2. e 3. b 4. c 5. a **C.** 1. only 2. went 3. forest 4. total 5. across 6. wrong 7. morning 8. different 9. summer, river **Page 49: D.** 1. c 2. b 3. b 4. c 5. a 6. a 7. c 8. a 9. c 10. b **E.** 1. different 2. went 3. across 4. forest 5. summer 6. total **F.** 1. d 2. a 3. e 4. b 5. c **Page 50: G.** 1. forest 2. morning 3. summer 4. river 5. total 6. went **H.** 1. in the summer 2. by a river 3. They went swimming. 4. They took a wrong path. 5. They saw five animals on the way back. 6. They enjoy being outside and seeing plants and animals.

LESSON 16

Page 51: A. 1. round 2. love 3. down 4. picture **B.** One Syllable: best, down, love, now, round, small; Two Syllables: after, carry, picture, winter **C.** 1. best 2. small 3. carry 4. now 5. love 6. round 7. picture 8. down 9. after, winter **Page 52: D.** 1. b 2. c 3. b 4. c 5. a 6. a 7. c 8. a 9. b 10. c **E.** 1. d 2. e 3. f 4. c 5. a 6. b **F.** 1. rest 2. clown 3. cow 4. hound 5. tall **Page 53: G.** 1. d 2. a 3. e 4. b 5. f 6. c **H.** 1. A boy named John. 2. It is winter. 3. They dress warmly and carry a backpack with food, water, and a camera. 4. He likes to take pictures. 5. He likes the contrast of the red fox against the white snow. 6. Possible: They enjoy them.

LESSON 17

Page 54: A. 1. wash 2. saw 3. laugh 4. guess **B.** 1. laughs, laughed, laughing 2. washing, washed, washes 3. shows, showing, showed 4. guessed, guesses, guessing **C.** 1. off 2. early 3. guess 4. most 5. saw 6. laugh 7. always 8. believe 9. show, wash **Page 55: D.** 1. c 2. a 3. a 4. b 5. c 6. b 7. b 8. a 9. b 10. c **E.** 1. yes 2. yes 3. yes 4. no 5. yes **F.** 1. show 2. early 3. wash 4. always 5. off 6. believe **Page 56: G.** 1. most 2. show 3. wash 4. believe 5. laugh 6. early **H.** 1. She is a pet dog. 2. She always comes when her food is out. 3. She can sit, lie down, and shake hands. 4. She lives in the country. 5. She was covered in purple. 6. Answers will vary.

LESSON 18

Page 57: A. 1. build 2. number 3. woman 4. office **B.** 1. great 2. son 3. hour **C.** 1. number 2. son 3. woman 4. around 5. beautiful 6. great 7. hour 8. build 9. funny, office **Page 58: D.** 1. c 2. a 3. b 4. a

5. c 6. c 7. a 8. b 9. c 10. b **E.** 1. c 2. e 3. f 4. b 5. a
6. d **F.** 1. fun 2. sunny 3. late
Page 59: G. 1. b 2. c 3. e 4. f 5. d 6. a **H.** 1. great
2. beautiful 3. woman 4. around 5. funny 6. son
7. hour 8. office 9. build 10. number

LESSON 19

Page 60: A. 1. never 2. high 3. true 4. year
5. company 6. reason **B.** 1.–4. every, learn, please,
soon **C.** 1. true 2. never 3. please 4. soon 5. high
6. year 7. learn 8. reason 9. company, every
Page 61: D. 1. b 2. a 3. a 4. b 5. c 6. c 7. b 8. a 9. c
10. b **E.** 1. high 2. please 3. year 4. learn 5. company
6. every **F.** Two Syllables: never, reason; Three
Syllables: every, company **Page 62: G.** 1. company
2. year 3. learn 4. never 5. high 6. please **H.** 1. a
brother or sister of Salim 2. He was on the top bunk.
3. He was asked to get dressed. 4. He was reading.
5. He should pay attention and do what is asked
of him. 6. Answers will vary. He was probably
embarrassed.

LESSON 20

Page 63: A. 1. hurt 2. long 3. visit 4. thought **B.** 1. b
2. d 3. f 4. e 5. a 6. c **C.** 1. thought 2. long 3. able
4. hurt 5. follow 6. doesn't 7. return 8. visit 9. better,
cover **Page 64: D.** 1. a 2. b 3. b 4. c 5. a 6. c 7. a
8. b 9. c 10. a **E.** 1. visited, visits, visiting 2. returns,
returned, returning 3. follows, followed, following
F. 1. yes 2. yes 3. no 4. no 5. yes **Page 65: G.** 1. better
2. cover 3. doesn't 4. visit 5. long 6. hurt **H.** 1. Lin
came to visit. 2. She thought Doug's questions were
rude. 3. She told him to be nice to Lin or she wouldn't
speak to him again. 4. He stayed out of their way.
5. She got tired of Lin following her around.
6. Answers will vary. He had been right to ask the
questions.

LESSON 21

Page 66: A. 1. smile 2. government **B.** One Syllable:
live, once, smile, thing, wear, which; Two Syllables:
minute; Three Syllables: another, government,
remember **C.** 1. thing 2. which 3. government 4. smile
5. minute 6. live 7. wear 8. once 9. another, remember
Page 67: D. 1. c 2. a 3. b 4. c 5. c 6. a 7. c 8. a 9. b
10. b **E.** 1. wear 2. which **F.** 1. give 2. dunce 3. pile
4. ring 5. bear 6. itch 7. September 8. mother

Page 68: G. 1. live 2. minute 3. remember 4. once
5. smile 6. government **H.** Answers may vary. Possible:
The topic is jobs a group of friends may someday
have. 2. He once visited Washington, D.C. 3. She
wants to wear beautiful clothes. 4. He wants to be a
comedian on TV. 5. He wants to be able to sleep late.
6. Answers will vary.

LESSON 22

Page 69: A. 1. start 2. world **B.** 1. c 2. e 3. f 4. a 5. d
6. b **C.** 1. start 2. kept 3. nothing 4. often 5. receive
6. enough 7. service 8. world 9. matter, together
Page 70: D. 1. b 2. a 3. b 4. c 5. b 6. a 7. b 8. a
9. b 10. a **E.** 1. nothing 2. enough 3. matter 4. world
5. start 6. together **F.** 1. enough 2. world 3. together
4. receive 5. matter 6. kept 7. nothing 8. often
Page 71: G. 1. d 2. a 3. e 4. c 5. f 6. b **H.** 1. It won't
start. 2. He thinks the car isn't getting enough gas.
3. He looks at the gas gauge. 4. He usually takes it
poorly. 5. It was his fault. 6. Answers will vary.

LESSON 23

Page 72: A. 1. first 2. second **B.** 1. fur 2. lung 3. worst
4. witty 5. clover 6. lure **C.** 1. pretty 2. young 3. today
4. except 5. were 6. second 7. sure 8. over 9. first,
yesterday **Page 73: D.** 1. c 2. a 3. b 4. c 5. c 6. b
7. a 8. c 9. a 10. b **E.** 1. c 2. e 3. f 4. a 5. b 6. d **F.** 1. yes
2. yes 3. no 4. no 5. yes 6. yes **Page 74: G.** 1. pretty
2. second 3. yesterday 4. first 5. young 6. today
H. 1. young 2. first 3. except 4. today 5. yesterday
6. were 7. over 8. pretty 9. second 10. sure

LESSON 24

Page 75: A. 1. next 2. among 3. won't 4. myself
5. until 6. those **B.** 1.–4. brought, might, tomorrow,
very **C.** 1. next 2. those 3. won't 4. very 5. tomorrow
6. myself 7. among 8. until 9, brought, might
Page 76: D. 1. a 2. b 3. a 4. c 5. c 6. b 7. c 8. b 9. c
10. a **E.** 1. myself 2. those 3. tomorrow 4. among
F. 1. text 2. light 3. thought 4. rose 5. berry 6. borrow
Page 77: G. 1. yes 2. yes 3. no 4. yes 5. yes 6. yes
H. 1. He or she brought things to sell at the fair.
2. The students were raising money for the next year's
team. 3. The team plays baseball. 4. They will know
tomorrow. 5. He or she will bake cupcakes. 6. Most
likely, it took place at school.